Aroma Heal 1

2nd Edition

Aroma Heal 1

Simple Techniques To Support Emotional Healing With Essential Oils
(2nd Edition of Original Title Aroma Heal)

Christi Turley Diamond B.S., M.Ed.
with
Karisa Tomkinson B.S., M.S.

iv

Disclaimer and Note to Readers

The material in this book is for informational purposes only. As each individual situation is unique, you should use proper discretion, in consultation with a health care practitioner, before undertaking the exercises and techniques described in this book. If you have any health problems, consult a doctor before using this book. The authors and publisher expressly disclaim responsibility for any adverse effects that may result from the use or application of the book. It is not intended to prescribe, or treat any emotional or physical condition, illness or injury. Application of oils is solely at the discretion of the reader and any direction given in the book is merely a guideline for its use. The authors, publishers or distributors of this book shall have no liability or responsibility to a person or entity with respect to any and all alleged damage, loss or injury caused or alleged to be caused directly or indirectly by the information contained in this book. This book contains suggested use of oils based on acceptable dosage amounts. The authors make no claim to have verified or validated these suggestions. The readers must validate acceptable dosage amounts from the manufacturer before application. The information in this book is in no way intended as a substitute for medical advice and the authors recommend that all readers obtain medical advice from a licensed healthcare professional before using essential oils for any reason.

Dedication

We dedicate this book to our children who light up our lives daily and inspire us to be better mothers and better women. They are the fire behind our passion for making the world a better place by assisting others to heal and live their passion and purpose. Our lives wouldn't be complete without the joy our amazing children bring us! We also want to dedicate this book to our husbands who are our sounding boards, our cheerleaders and our best friends. This could not have been accomplished without their love and support for us! We love you Rick and Tyler!

Table of Contents:

Preface

This book was written not as a cure-all, but as a helpful guide with tools and suggestions for supporting emotional healing. First, we introduce you to essential oils and the chemistry behind why they help emotionally. We then talk about healing on an energetic level. Both are effective modalities in healing, but combined are even more impressive and powerful. Many people want to know how to effectively combine the two, so this is an introduction into that very topic. We will introduce you to several techniques and exercises later on in the book that combine both essential oils and energetic healing in support of emotional healing. They will have step-by-step instructions on how to use them to your benefit. All the information contained within is provided to give you specific, powerful, useful tools to help you grow and heal.

Aroma Heal 1

2nd Edition

Introduction: Christi's Experience

Over the course of the last few years, I have been drawn to the world of energy healing and the powerful effect it can have on emotional healing. Energy healing came seeking me rather than me seeking it. Time and again, I have seen what it can do in changing lives. When I do sessions with my clients, we are able to release false beliefs and trapped emotions that have plagued them for years. Releasing emotions tied to issues that have blocked them from progressing helps them gain a new lease on life. I call these "energy blocks." Energy blocks are the unresolved issues or emotions that were never completely released, processed, cleared or healed. They have been bottled up in the body; needing to get out because of damage done emotionally and physically to a person's wellbeing.

I received emotional healing myself from energy work. Having experienced physical abuse and a painful divorce, I had participated in counseling over the course of a few years. My counselor was amazing and insightful and progress was made with great clarity. Skeptical and naïve about energy healing, I was curious to see what it could do for me as well. Just after one session I was amazed at the lightness I experienced afterwards and a great sense of healing. It was like I could feel my spirit breathe again.

Counseling had helped me put the puzzle pieces together but the energy healing helped me dig to the root and release where the pain began in the first place. I felt like I was removing the rocks that had built a wall around my heart and as I progressively released more and more over time, the light from my soul began to shine through and feel strong again. It was life changing for me and pivotal in helping me get in tune to my spirit and who I really am. I saw permanent results without having to reiterate the trauma and relive it. I wanted others to experience what I had so I delved further into studying energy healing and light work. The healing was quick and transformational with huge results. I then began my own journey as a facilitator and studied under some gifted and incredible mentors who educated me on how and why it works and how it goes to a deep energetic and spiritual level. I invested myself in intense training and eventually began doing sessions with my own clients.

I have seen powerful transformation in clients as I work with them in sessions for their own energetic healing. The results have been remarkable and quick. I worked with a woman to release some deep painful experiences and emotions she had held onto for 20 years and literally saw her countenance change as she released this. It helped her in moving forward in her relationships. I worked with a gentleman who was grieving the loss of two of his sisters who had died within months of each other feel more complete and whole afterwards. Much progress can be done in just one session, but over a period of time, real transformation occurs. At first subtly, and then gradually, a deeper and more defined healing seems to take place.

I felt prompted a while back to start looking into essential oils. I had heard of essential oils but never really delved into them or knew what they could do. So, one summer I studied them in depth. I happened to be experiencing a very painful and emotionally draining situation that summer that was affecting me physically. I felt depressed and at the suggestion of one of my mentors I began using the oils on myself. I began taking them internally and also using them topically. I combined the use of the essential oils with releasing some of the pain and emotions through energy healing and started to see a great difference in how I felt. After using the oils over a short period of time, I felt a palpable calmness surround me. I felt more grounded and my depression dissipated. I was amazed at the results. I want to stress that this was my personal experience with them. I am not claiming they will always do the same for everyone.

I studied the oils' emotional properties and had another personal epiphany. Due to the painful traumatic experience and process I was going through, I felt a lot of grief and a great sense of loss. I decided to go away for a weekend with my husband to take a breather and have some time to process and heal. While we were away, we took out my collection of essential oils and muscle tested to see which oils would benefit us the most. We then used them for a massage on each other.

One of the oils that came up for me, as we were testing them, was Rosemary. Rosemary essential oil supports one in feeling confident during times of great change and helps with grief. I was prepared to release pain and accept healing. As my husband rubbed Rosemary oil on my back, I felt a wave of grief overcome me and wash away the pain that had been bottled up. It allowed me the emotional release I needed to let go of the loss. I shed a few tears as I released some very agonizing feelings and then relaxed, breathed in the healing, and felt so empowered. This was a significant moment for me.

Soon after, I started diffusing the oils as aromatherapy and using them in my sessions with my clients. I would tune into what emotions or experiences they wanted to work on and release. I would diffuse the oil most beneficial to that emotional release in order to support them. Then, I would suggest they apply the same oil topically on their wrists and breathe it in while they were in sessions with me. I feel it helped the sessions go even smoother and supported the work we were doing to release and heal. It was empowering for them to be able to take the oils home and apply them as we had during the session, or even take some internally (not ALL essential oils are safe to ingest so please take proper precautions to educate yourself on which ones are labeled as safe to ingest and which ones aren't before doing so), to help them further progress their healing. I saw great results! I realized the oils were creating a supportive environment for the body in its emotional healing as the energetic blocks loosened up and released quicker. It's the difference between trying to scrape dried up paint off of your hands by just rubbing and peeling and hoping you get it all as opposed to putting water on the paint first to loosen it up so it comes off easier and quicker. The essential oils become the water to loosen up the emotions that have been stuck for years and loosen them up to be released with more ease and no residue, making the healing an easier process.

I now use many processes with my clients in helping them create healing in all aspects of their lives whether it be emotional, physical, financially or in their relationships and that is why I created www.thehealingcoach.com to provide a way for people to find their own inner healing that is powerful, efficient and effective.

Karisa's Story

Karisa's experiences after being introduced to essential oils

Last summer began one of the most challenging experiences of my life. It challenged my trust in those closest and dearest to me. I felt hardened and distanced from those I loved most. I felt very dishonored and, in a way, sacrificed. I immersed myself in the faith of my religious understanding for comfort and guidance. During this time, I was prompted to use essential oils in my life. I had never experienced them before nor knew anything about them. I acted solely on this new inspiration.

About a month after I began using the essential oils, I received a specific blend as an inspired gift from a mentor of mine. I loved this oil blend from the moment I opened the bottle. The smell was calming, and seemed to embrace my soul in love and understanding for myself as well as those I was in this present challenge with. I used this oil daily. I felt my heart opening up. My understanding of the situation itself grew. It was so beautiful to feel a transformation from the feelings of sadness, sorrow, and dishonor to an increase in compassion, respect, and affection. My children even referred to it as my 'happy oil'. The conflict wasn't resolved completely, but my perspective had shifted. I had grown in my understanding, easing the weight on my soul significantly.

About three months later though, I found that I wasn't so drawn to the scent of this oil. I no longer felt the need or desire for its daily use. I was confused. Why didn't I love it anymore? So, I turned to my box of essential oils I had collected. I felt prompted to open a different essential oil…--the one that had been the most disgusting smelling oil to me the month before when I'd received it! I was so confused as to why I was feeling that I needed to open this bottle of essential oil that had previously smelled awful to me. I followed this odd-seeming prompting though and found it had a completely different smell to me this time. Instead of offensive, it smelled inviting and I was drawn to it. I found myself wanting to apply it and wear it daily. The drastic change intrigued me, so I began to do some research into the oils.

The initial oil I had been given as a gift was an essential oil blend of Lavender, Sweet Marjoram, Roman Chamomile, Ylang Ylang, Sandalwood, and Vanilla Bean extract. This blend of oils aids in softening the heart of hard, resentful emotions that block it like a wall would. As this wall is removed, it opens up a space to fully forgive and receive love. I used this oil for a period of about three months as I healed emotionally and was able to resolve those negative emotions and forgive completely. The second oil I was drawn to was Geranium essential oil. This oil fosters feelings of connectedness such as those of belief, conviction, credence, and unconditional love while addressing non-beneficial emotions such as loss, heavy hearted-ness, and grief. I saw a direct progression in my emotional healing. The oil blend that addressed the bitter and resentful emotions helped me to work through those emotions completely before I could effectively address the feelings of loss and grief. It was a direct correlation to the emotional healing process. Once I realized this, with a heart full of gratitude and tears in my eyes, I became deeply interested in the emotional healing component to essential oils. My body and mind were able to acknowledge what I needed from the essential oils without my being aware of the reasons why.

Essential Oils and Emotions

Essential oils have been around since the beginning of time. Their healing properties are very powerful. Essential oils do not do the healing but rather are used for helping the body do what it was meant to do naturally: heal itself. Essential oils are becoming mainstream as people become more aware of the scientific evidence in how effective they are in supporting the body with its natural healing properties. Certain odor molecules, when inhaled as with aromatherapy, enter the blood stream and circulate through the body. This process seems to occur within a few short minutes after application and can continue to occur for up to 24 hours.

The therapeutic benefits of essential oils are primarily based on their chemical make-up--the *constituents* that comprise it. These chemical constituents can have unique capabilities and produce effects that can stimulate, reduce inflammation, inhibit bacteria, calm, regenerate, etc. For example, esters are a grouping of constituents that balance and soothe. Essential oils such as lavender, clary sage, geranium, and Roman chamomile are examples of oils that contain esters. Oxides have expectorant qualities, which make them beneficial for colds and congestion. Some examples of essential oils containing oxides are melaleuca, eucalyptus, and rosemary. Aldehydes are constituents that reduce inflammation and are calming and can be found in lemongrass and Melissa oil. Each oil contains certain chemical constituents which is why each varies in its physical and emotional benefits.

Essential oils are also effective in assisting the body to heal emotionally. The emotional part of the brain is the limbic system and this is where they do their work through the sense of smell. Following is an explanation as to how essential oils support emotional healing through aromatherapy.

What is Aromatherapy?

Our sense of smell is a very powerful tool. When we smell something, it can elicit very strong emotional and/or physical reactions. There is a scientific explanation for this. When we smell something, it stimulates the olfactory cells that are part of the olfactory system and, the information travels to five different brain structures, including the amygdala. The amygdala is the part of the brain that is responsible for storing and releasing emotional trauma. Anatomically, the olfactory system is closely related to the limbic system of the brain which is responsible for long-term memory, emotions, autonomic nervous system, regulating blood pressure, heart-rate, and attention. The close proximity between the olfactory and limbic systems is why essential oils have such a profound effect physiologically and psychologically. As we inhale the oils through aromatherapy, the emotional parts of our brain are affected.

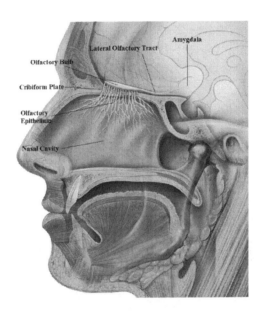

How do essential oils work with our emotions?

- Certain essential oils work by calming the central nervous system and helping us to relax instead of allowing the build-up of anxiety in the body.

Anxiety can actually create an acidic condition in the body, which activates an enzyme that results in the anxiety being stored in the DNA.

- Essential oils can be useful in releasing old emotional traumas. In 1989, Dr. Joseph Ledoux, from NY Medical University, discovered that the amygdala (in the limbic center of the brain) plays a role in the storage and release of emotional traumas. He also suggested that aromas could trigger an emotional release.[1]

- Essential oils carry molecules known as sesquiterpenes, which are capable of penetrating the blood-brain barrier. The molecules carried have a significant oxygenating effect on the brain. The combination of the stimulation from aromatic molecules and the oxygenation on the brain appears to assist the amygdala in supporting the release of emotional blockages.

- Essential oils can even help to affect emotions trapped within various organs and tissues of the body.[2]

- Essential oils can also help balance and raise our frequencies, therefore having an effect on the human energy field.

Scientific research has shown that everything has a frequency, including emotions. Robert O Becker, M.D., documented the electrical frequency of the human body in the book, *The Body Electric*.

Measurements were taken in Mega Hertz. The healthy human body has a frequency that sits in a range of between 62-68 MHz. Sickness and disease begin to kick in when the body's frequency decreases to 58 MHz. In the 1990s, Bruce Tainio developed equipment to measure the bio-frequency of humans and foods. The tables below by C & A Higley show the range of frequencies found amongst both.

Frequency Of People and Things	MHz
Human Brain	72-90 MHz
Human Body (Day)	62-68 MHz
Cold Symptoms	58 MHz
Flu Symptoms	57 MHz
Candida	55 MHz
Epstein-Barr	52 MHz
Cancer	42 MHz
Onset of Death	25 MHz
Processed Canned Food	0 MHz
Fresh Produce	Up to 15MHz
Dry Herbs	12-22 MHz
Fresh Herbs	20-27 MHz
Essential Oils	52-320 MHz

Frequency of People and Things Data from the Reference Guide to Essential Oils by C&A Higley

Essential oils were found to have the highest frequency of any natural substance used by 'man.' When placed on or in the body, essential oils, in their purest forms, can raise the vibration of the human body. Specific vibrations are as follows:

Frequency Of Single Essential Oils	MHz
Rose	320 MHz
Helichrysum	181 MHz
Frankincense	147 MHz
Ravensara	134 MHz
Lavender	118 MHz
German Chamomile	105 MHz
Idaho Tansy	105 MHz
Myrrh	105 MHz
Melissa	102 MHz
Juniper	98 MHz
Sandalwood	96 MHz
Angelica	85 MHz
Peppermint	78 MHz
Galbanum	56 MHz
Basil	52 MHz

Frequency of Essential Oils Data from the Reference Guide to Essential Oils by C&A Higley

Karisa's Story Continues

Life was moving along beautifully, and then I got stuck. I just didn't feel like I could progress despite all my efforts. I was trying hard to grow my business by following the techniques my mentors and business coaches provided me with, but instead, it was regressing. I was connecting with my Creator regularly through meditation, prayer, and study, but was stumped. I was going out of my way to do those things that have always brought progression before, but I didn't feel I was moving anywhere. I felt a sense of overwhelm from all this stagnancy, despite working so very hard. In the midst of this, I felt inspired to contact Christi Diamond. We had never met before, but were contacts on Facebook through a mutual mentor. I messaged her and within the week we had a session scheduled to do energy healing. I had absolutely no idea what this experience would entail, but I knew through my personal meditation and prayer that it was what I needed to do next.

I was in tears our entire first session, simply because I felt the healing power from following the promptings I'd received. Throughout the session, I felt like Christi was giving me keys to doors that I had seen, but had not been able to open. I had an idea of what was behind the doors, but as soon as I was able to open them, the peace and joy that really filled the place in my heart was overwhelming. I had all the answers within myself all along, but she was able to help me access them through her work and by incorporating several of the techniques taught and explained in this book.

My business quadrupled in growth the two weeks following that session. My peace and personal understanding was clearer.

I set up another session with her for a few weeks later. Before that second session, I went to my special box of essential oils. It had been an emotionally rough day and I made sure to put on an essential oil blend to repel non-beneficial energy and also Roman Chamomile, to help gain more insight to my own spiritual mission and purpose. It was another beautiful session. When I went to put on those same oils before bed though, I found that I wasn't drawn to the oil blend that repelled negativity or non-beneficial energy at all. I was initially (and briefly) surprised by this, because it was a favorite of mine. I realized quickly that through completing the energy work with Christi, we had been able to clear away the negativity and non-beneficial energy and I no longer needed assistance from that particular oil blend.

The experience reinforced to me the value of the energy work in combination with the oils. I was able to make immediate and impacting progress in my personal, emotional, and financial circumstances by combining them. My first experience with oils had taken several months for the emotional healing to occur, whereas, when the essential oils were combined with the power of energy work, the results felt almost instantaneous. That is where and when I found my passion for the combination of energy work and essential oils for emotional healing.

Healing Energetically

Now that we have touched a little on why essential oils help emotionally, let's delve into healing energetically. People often walk around carrying false beliefs. For instance, let's say that as a child, I was taught I was worthless. If I held that thought in my head constantly, how do you think I would act? WORTHLESS. I wouldn't try hard at anything, because I would already know that I was going to fail anyway. I would teach others to treat me as worthless, because I had no confidence in myself. My life would continue in a negative cycle, because of a false belief I bought into as a child from the adult figures in my life.

Let's examine the other side of the spectrum. What if I held the belief that I was limitless? I would probably believe that I could do anything. In contrast, how would I live my life with this belief? I would think I could accomplish anything, so I would probably be unstoppable, right? I would push past my limits and I would continuously make great things happen in my life. Our beliefs shape who we are, what we become, and mold our lives daily.

How do we clear out those false beliefs that were planted early and cause us so much harm? Well, we have emotions that are attached to those beliefs;

emotions tied to painful or traumatic experiences in our lives. Those emotions have non-beneficial energy attached to them and can wreak havoc on us physically, spiritually, and emotionally. In order to clear them away, the fastest and most effective way is to energetically release them.

Restoring balance to our lives starts at a cellular level. We are made up of our ancestors' DNA, which records information and manifests it in our physical form. Sometimes patterns are passed on to us generationally that we aren't even aware of. Some of those patterns can be non-beneficial. An example is when a person had the false belief that they are eternally indebted to someone, causing them to always feel the need to give excessively of their time, efforts, or things till they are worn, tired, and weak. (Sound like a mother or other female figure you know?) This false belief isn't beneficial in any way. It impedes the individual from being able to serve to the capacity they desire. It's like putting the airplane oxygen mask on a child without ever reaching for your own.

We also have life experiences that were never fully processed or grieved or false beliefs that we hold onto that don't serve us in a positive manner. There could be experiences in our past: a loss that we experienced, the death of a loved one or even current relationships that continue to cause us pain.

Just as we need to clear our homes of non-beneficial energy, it is important to also clear our hearts from non-beneficial experiences that may have been very painful. We need to clear out the non-beneficial energy and clean the space it is taking in our heart. Some of these experiences can also be from our childhood. When we have non-beneficial energy hanging around in our hearts, it is necessary to replace that non-beneficial energy with the energy of love, light, and joy. This is what makes love so powerful! It has the ability to wash away the negativity that is stuck in our minds. Love is a constantly moving and changing source of energy. Love does not change from its pure form, but rather grows and manifests with the experiences and relationships we obtain. Stagnant or non-beneficial energy stays in one place. It only changes or moves with our own will. If we choose to stay ignorant of stagnant energy, we make a conscious choice to not heal and to not love. Therefore we create physical ailments, illnesses, and diseases. Our bodies are literally a reflection and manifestation of the deepest parts of our being.

"Unacknowledged feelings from past experiences are stored in the body and then unconsciously

have a powerful effect on who you are, how you behave, and how you feel about yourself. Using the body as the gateway to awareness, buried feelings and memories can surface, freeing us from old patterns and energy blocks that keep us feeling stuck and unable to live life to its fullest."
--Bodymind[3]

So, how do we use the body as a gateway to increase the awareness of our buried feelings and our pain? How do we use it to our benefit to cleanse us and help us heal? Well, the healing properties of essential oils, when combined with the techniques that assist in healing at the energetic level, create a powerful tool. When I work with my clients, I do delve deeper using my gifts, incorporating various tools and techniques, and help release on a deeper emotional level. Some of these tools and techniques I use, as simple as they are, are powerfully effective. As we continue, we will explain how to personally implement them.

Essential oils are one tool to aid in the emotional healing process. They help the emotions, feelings, and issues to surface so that the individual can better work through each part of them fully. As explained, earlier, when we smell something, it is because we absorb scent molecules. The molecules bind to sensors in the nose and travel to the amygdala (and four other locations) in the brain. The amygdala is responsible for storing and releasing emotional trauma. That is why specific smells can recall such strong emotions and memories.

Knowing that healing starts at the cellular level of our physical being, we must incorporate physical tools that truly affect our body. Pure essential oils have healing properties that work instantaneously. Our body absorbs these oils naturally and breaks them down into our cells, adding their life-enhancing properties. These oils are made from plants, created from the natural elements of the earth.

We are constantly affected by our surroundings through sound, sight, taste, touch, and scent. Oils can definitely make a difference when applied to our skin, inhaled through aromatherapy, and used internally (only some oils are safe to ingest). Essential oils work from the inside out by getting rid of a sickness very similarly to the way an antibiotic would. Combining the healing power of the essential oils with our own power to heal, we can begin to release the emotions from the past and let go of painful experiences by remembering the following:

- We are going to focus on those things that come up for us and seem to stay in our energy field that keep the pain and anger there.

- We know how powerful our thoughts can be and the power we have over them. Controlling our thoughts and giving ourselves the freedom to truly heal is the key.

- We have the power to heal ourselves of experiences that were painful and traumatic for us and let go of them, so that they no longer hold any power over us.

- This process and growth gives us more freedom to live our lives authentically and live powerfully in our purpose.

"When you change the way you look at things, the things you look at change."
Wayne Dyer, PhD

Healing Tools
&
Techniques

Methods of Essential Oil Application

Before using essential oils, it is important to educate yourself on the application of them and the variety of ways to do so. The essential oils that we work with are very pure and therapeutic grade. We would caution that you look at the label of any essential oil you might use to see if it is safe for ingestion or for topical use on the skin before using it in either way. The oils we use are in their purest form and very safe and effective. We would even go as far as saying that the purest form of essential oils you can find will be the most effective in helping emotionally because the purer they are, the higher the frequency and effectiveness in doing what they are supposed to in order to support your body in its natural way of healing physically and emotionally. You will have far better results with the purest forms of essential oils. This is pertinent.

Topically

Direct application onto the skin is one of the easiest ways to use essential oils. It is highly effective since essential oils can easily pass through the lipid membranes of cell walls. They are able to penetrate cells and disperse throughout the body within seconds. It is because there are SO many nerve endings from the entire body are found there. Think of reflexology. You are able to safely access most parts of the body from one location via the nervous system.

Before you start, remember to test a small area of the skin first. Apply one oil or blend at a time. When layering oils that are new to you, allow 2-3 minutes between each oil application to give the body a chance to respond before applying a second oil.

The longer that essential oils stay in contact with the skin, the more likely they are to be absorbed. Don't wash them off too soon.

Carrier oils are organic oils that are used to carry the oil to a greater surface area of the skin. When massaging, the carrier oil helps lubricate the skin, as well. These can easily be found at a local grocery or health foods store. Some suggested carrier oils are:

- Olive Oil
- Coconut Oil
- Sesame Oil
- Wheat Germ Oil
- Almond Oil
- Grapeseed (cold-pressed) Oil
- Jojoba Oil

When applying essential oils to children, always use a carrier oil. Lavender oil does not require dilution as long as it is not lavandin or genetically-engineered lavender. Add 15-30 drops of essential oil to one ounce of a quality carrier oil and mix well.

How to Dispense Essential Oil

Hold the bottle of oil 1 to 4 inches above the fingers or palm of the other hand. Tip the bottle over and wait for the oil to drip out. Then, massage the oil onto the desired area. Oil can also be dropped directly over the body in this way, such as the back or other parts of the body.

Some essential oils are thicker than others and require a gentle shake. Make sure to never touch the center of the drop dispenser -- let the oil drip from the edge freely. This ensures that the pure essential oil remaining in the bottle is not contaminated by the oils from your skin.

Layering

Multiple oils can be applied, one at a time, using a technique called layering. For example, if marjoram is used on a sore muscle; it is massaged into the tissue until the area is dry. Then the next oil is applied - perhaps lemongrass, until the oil is absorbed. Then the third oil, possibly basil, until the oil is absorbed. This step can be continued with as many oils as necessary or desired.

Massage

Mix 3-4 drops of essential oil with ½ tsp. of a massage oil blend or carrier oil to create custom massage oil. Whenever you go get a massage, have the massage therapist add some essential oils to their massage oil or lotion and experience a massage like no other!

Diffusing/Aromatherapy

Diffusing essential oils is a perfect way to improve your home, work, or living environment. Diffusing can purify the air and neutralize mildew, cigarette smoke or other odors, as well as protect you and your family from viruses and bacteria.

Inhalation/Aromatherapy Techniques

- Place 2 or more drops into the palm of one hand and rub your hands together. Cup hands together over the nose and mouth and inhale deeply.

- Place 2 or 3 drops of essential oil in a cool mist diffuser in a room in your home.

- Add several drops of an essential oil to a bowl of hot (not boiling) water. Inhale the vapors that rise from the bowl. A towel can be placed over the head and bowl to increase the intensity of the vapors.

- Apply a few drops of essential oil to a cotton ball, tissue, natural-fiber handkerchief, or clay necklace and inhale periodically.

- Apply 2 or more drops of oil anywhere on your upper body, such as chest, neck, sternum, under nose and ears or wrists. Breathe in the fragrance throughout the day.

Breathing

We've just covered the essential oil use. Since we are using aromatherapy with the oils, we have already discussed how it affects the emotional part of the brain through smell. Let's now discuss breathing and how important that is in relaxing and healing and the significance of breathing in through the nose, before we go to the healing techniques.

Controlled breathing not only keeps the mind and body functioning at their best, it can also lower blood pressure, promote feelings of calm and relaxation, and—if we play our lungs right— help us de-stress.

Two of the many reasons breathing is important is because it supplies our bodies and organs with the oxygen necessary for survival, and it rids our bodies of waste products. Oxygen is essential for our brain, glands, nerves, and internal organs. If the brain is deprived of oxygen, it can damage other organs and systems in our bodies. Lack of oxygen is a major cause of heart disease, strokes, and cancer.

I have noticed that when I am experiencing emotions of overwhelm, frustration, anxiety, and stress, my breathing becomes strained. I wasn't even aware of the physical response my body was expressing until a friend pointed this out to me. I would rest between breaths and then just take deep, exacerbated breaths. It wasn't an even, calm, breathing pattern. My breathing was directly correlating with the stressed emotions I was experiencing.

Breathing is literally vital to our physical health, but it also correlates closely with our emotions. Our body responds physically to our emotions whether we are aware of it or not, and our emotions are affected by our physical body in return.

When I became aware of my strained breathing, I paused and took a few moments to focus on relaxing my breathing. I focused on my body's physical response and on each inhale and exhale so that they flowed continuously, rhythmically, and relaxed.

Once my breathing was under control, I realized that my emotions had settled significantly as well. My mind was calmer. I didn't feel as if I were emotionally drowning and 'gasping' for air. I had figuratively stood up in the water I felt I was drowning in, and was able to calmly recognize the solutions, direction, and peace that had been available to me the whole time.

Progressive Relaxation

The type of breathing technique to become familiar with using these tools and with Aromatherapy is called ***Progressive Relaxation.***

How it's done: To let go of tension from head to toe, close your eyes and focus on tensing and relaxing each muscle group for two to three seconds each. Start with the feet and toes, then move up to the knees, thighs, rear, chest, arms, hands, neck, jaw, and eyes—all while maintaining deep, slow breaths. Having trouble staying on track? Anxiety and panic specialist Dr. Patricia Farrell suggests we breathe in through the nose, hold for a count of five while the muscles tense, and then breathe out through the mouth on release.[4] The key is to progressively relax with each breath and releasing tension from each muscle until your whole body feels calm and stress free.

Healing Environment

The following tools will be very helpful in clearing yourself of non-beneficial energy and past experiences that may have carried pain with them. There are guidelines to using these tools to achieve maximum benefit. Make sure to give yourself plenty of time to use the tools. If you are teaching these techniques to others, either one on one or in a group setting, make sure to allow for plenty of time to relax and then process the tools so that there is a feeling of completeness in using the process. I want to stress how important it is that these exercises are performed in a quiet space away from noise and distractions, so that you can completely process what you need to. I also want to encourage you to let feelings flow and to allow tears to flow if they need to. It's important to feel the emotions that arise from doing these exercises; it is part of the releasing process. I would encourage you to do the exercises on yourself first so you can experience their healing power and practice them on people close to you until you feel comfortable performing them in a class with others.

Visualization is necessary to heal energetically, and to connect the mind with the body. Each of these exercises requires you to close your eyes for most of the duration in order for the process to feel complete. It is recommended that you read through each exercise before actually performing it to familiarize yourself with it. You may feel more comfortable having someone read it for you and guiding you through it. Each exercise has been voice recorded for your convenience and to support you in doing some of these simple yet effective tools in a one on one or a group/class setting. To obtain the FREE RECORDINGS as our gift to you with your book purchase, please go to www.aromaheal.org.

We have shared some of our own experiences with energy healing and have educated you about how essential oils can heal. We then guided you through the stages of healing, the proper use of essential oils and breathing techniques. These are all pieces to the puzzle that encompass inner healing. Now it's time to fit it all together. As you go through each exercise, you will see the different layers of healing yourself, as you use each exercise to help heal emotions and experiences within you. Each exercise is designed to be simple and easy to use in the comfort of your own home. The reason we wrote this book was to literally bring healing to the world by empowering people to start taking healing into their own hands. These simple techniques are great beginners' tools in doing so. We acknowledge that more in depth healing can be accomplished through more intensive energy healing sessions, but also assure you that these tools provide a great start on the road to empowering you in your own healing. We have each experienced our own healing from these exercises and are excited to share these with the world.

As these tools have been successfully used on my clients and in workshops, I will include their testimonials in each section. Each exercise is described in a step by step process, so you can easily use them for yourself and those close to you. As you experience them, you will see subtle emotional changes within you, and possibly healing on a deep level. Effects vary from person to person, in part based on how prepared you feel you are to heal and let go.

* * *

Before getting started with any of the following tools or techniques, make sure to give yourself a measurement as to where you are at with the issue you are facing or seeking healing in. Rate yourself a number on a scale of 1-10 (with ten being closer to love, light, and peace, and one being farther from it) as to where you are at with the issue. After completing a healing tool, recheck yourself again to see where you are at and if the number has increased.

Healing Tool #1

Assessing the Relationships in Our Lives

This tool is helpful in letting go of past relationships that no longer serve you, present relationships that still continue to cause pain and require growth to move forward, relationships that hold you back, and helpful for letting go of relationships of the past or with those who have passed on and experiences or issues that tend to make you feel as though you can't let go.

When we look at the relationships in our lives, it is important to look at what these relationships do to us and for us. Are they beneficial to our lives and our purpose? Do they give our lives more fulfillment and meaning? The meaningful relationships in our lives shouldn't take away from us in order to be in them. Ask yourself, *How much is this relationship costing me to be in it?* When my own relationships tend to take away from my life and my purpose, I have to assess how much I want to further invest in those relationships.

The most fulfilling relationships are those based on complete truth, honesty, and a mutual respect for one another, with giving and receiving on both ends.

Our relationships should not deplete us of our energy, where we are a constant source of giving without receiving from the other end. Our relationships should give us love and fulfillment. Take inventory of the relationships in your life and what you receive from each of them and decide on those that are beneficial and rewarding. If there is conflict in some, then look at the cost that relationship may be to you. We can choose to be in a relationship with someone and still love them in the place and space that they are in, but we do not have to agree to unhealthy boundaries. We can love them from a distance if we have to for a while, but always look at which relationships in your life are fulfilling for yourself and others.

After assessing your relationships, here is an exercise to help you in letting go of the negative and strengthening the positive within them.

Cutting Cords and Energetic Strings

When we enter relationships, we start building energetic connections with people. Those connections continue to increase as the amount of time spent in the relationship increases. As time goes on, more energetic connections are made which can be beneficial or non-beneficial. A beneficial energetic connection between you and another person may be the time you spend together as a couple and the laughter you share together. A non-beneficial energetic connection might be a time when that person lied to you and broke a trust and continued to be dishonest. Some of these connections continue to tarnish our relationships or hold us in the past and keep us from growing in the relationship or moving forward in our lives after a relationship has ended.

These forms of energetic connections/cords exist in every relationship whether it's a parent, spouse, child, friend, co-workers etc. There could also be energetic connections you have with people in your life that traumatized you. We can likewise have energetic connections to money, weight and health issues and even material things.

This exercise requires your eyes to be closed for the duration. You might want to read through it first and familiarize yourself with the process or have someone read it for you and guide you through it. It is simple yet effective.

It is important that you set aside a little time for this exercise--maybe 2 or 5 minutes for each person that you need to heal your ties and connections to. Make sure you are in a quiet place with no interruptions and that you allow your feelings to flow freely. You can either sit in a comfortable chair for this or stand in a relaxed position; whichever suits you. This can be a wonderfully freeing experience.

Essential Oils needed for this healing tool:

Ginger –

Ginger essential oil compels an individual to fully participate and hold responsibility for their life, choices, and consequences. It empowers individuals to feel in control of their life and not to have a 'victim' mentality. It allows individuals to see that they are the creator of their own life.

Clove –

This oil is known to support healthy boundaries in all ways- energetically, emotionally, and mentally. This includes encouraging healthy independent relationships with others as well, allowing us to honor ourselves. It helps us to identify how we, or others, are sabotaging us and enables us to take a step forward towards empowering ourselves, freeing us from the feeling of victimization.

Melaleuca –

This oil is known to support and encourage healthy energetic boundaries. It is beneficial when dealing toxic, codependent, negative, or draining relationships. It is an oil that also helps us to identify areas or relationships, with others or ourselves, where we are unfocused, unbalanced, or even limiting ourselves.

Oregano –

Oregano essential oil is very powerful both physically and emotionally. It helps to soften the stubborn and strong willed so they are able to more clearly envision their higher purpose and connect to it. It helps to knock down those personal roadblocks so that one can move forward with more ease in collaboration with others. This is oil is beneficial in letting go of low vibration emotions and non beneficial energy. It can help to release deep seeded anger issues. Please note that Oregano is a 'hot' oil and such should always be diluted when being used. Use it with caution.

To purchase essential oils used in this book go to www.aromaheal.org

Exercise

(This exercise is recorded for your convenience and use. Please obtain your free download of the recording at www.AromaHeal.org.)

Mix 2 drops of each oil except for Oregano (use one drop of it) with 1 tsp of virgin or fractionated coconut oil and apply to the bottom of both feet. Feel free to diffuse the oils as well. It is fine to have several different oils in the diffuser. (Would not recommend Oregano in the diffuser)

Intention is a very important part of healing. Before using each tool, set your intention to what you want to create with it. For example, before this exercise I would say "My intention is to find healing in every relationship I address today." After setting and speaking your intention take 3 deep breaths and relax.

Think of a relationship in your life that you deserve some healing or closure with. (It is recommended to do this with one relationship or issue at a time.)

With your eyes closed, picture yourself standing in front of a person or issue. Picture all of the ties, cords, strings and connections between you that you share and that are connected to your relationship with this person. Or if it is something materialistic, or a traumatic experience, or an issue, picture that experience in front of you in a box with everything that is associated with it in any way. **Pause.**

Observe all the energetic cords formed between you two and be sure to include all the ties-- healthy and unhealthy. **Pause**.

Now you are going to cinch them all together and hold them in your hand and make sure you grab a hold of all of them; the good, the bad, and the ugly. You are now going to cut all these energetic ties between the two of you. Picture a large pair of scissors in your hands. These are a very special pair of scissors. They are white and full of love and light and healing. Picture the scissors in your hand. **Pause.**

Cutting cords doesn't mean, "I don't love you or care about you anymore." Cord cutting doesn't necessarily lead to break-ups or abandoned relationships. It simply means that you are releasing the dysfunctional parts of your relationships.

> *"Remember, fear is the opposite of love, and etheric cords (and all attachments) are created from fear." --Doreen Virtue*

Now take the scissors and cut every single cord between you until each one is severed. **Pause.**

After you have cut all the cords, strings and ties between you, you will gather all the cut ends on your side and hold them up above you to the light and healing power that comes from the God of your understanding. As you hold those up, picture white light surrounding all the severed ends and that a great healing is taking place and as it is all the cords completely dissolve and disappear. They are gone and no longer have a hold on you. **Pause.**

As you do this, now picture the person or issue you have just cut ties and cords with and have them hold up their cut ends to the light as well. Picture the white light and healing on their ends as well as their ends of the cords disappear. **Pause**

All that was between you is now healed and all the healthy cords that need to be there between you will reconnect in a more healing way. All the unhealthy cords have disappeared and are no longer between you two. All the ties, connections, and strings are now healed, good, and healthy ones and can reconnect if need be. Take one of the bottles of oils you have just used and breathe in the aroma of it. **Pause**

Out loud or in your mind say "I release the energetic hold these cords have had on me and I empower myself with healing". Tap your stomach 3 times and say, "Accept. Accept. Accept. Forever with me." This helps to integrate the healing into one of the main energy systems in your body.

You can now open your eyes.

Go through this process and repeat it for any relationships you feel you need healing in, until you have covered all the relationships and issues you need to heal.

Testimonials

"Cutting cords was such a turning point for me in my healing and letting go of a really painful relationship that continued to cause me pain even though it was over. The relationship I experienced was so unhealthy yet I couldn't seem to let go of the hold it had on me. When I pictured my ex in front of me, I could see so many cords between us and when I finally cut the cords, I felt a wave of relief come over me and felt the strong hold it had on me go away. It was so simple and so freeing!! I love this exercise and now I use it all the time! I even used it to cut cords between me and my childhood home that had so many bad memories for me. I'm so grateful for Christi teaching this to me!"

"I used this exercise to cut cords with everyone in my life! Sounds scary and it was at first but when I realized I was really cutting out all the unhealthy cords I had with everyone and allowing more space for healthy ones to form, I just went to town and cleared them all for everyone in my life and it felt amazing. It's like a weight lifted from me and I felt more energized and free to have better relationships with each person!"

Healing Tool #2

Who Are You?

If our energy is focused on the past, we aren't able to put our energy into the present moment and live fully and authentically. We are allowing our pain of the past to define us. Experiences from the past have shaped us, but we are the ones who decide how much power these experiences either teach us or defeat and define us. If I am divorced, I do not define myself as being divorced and introduce myself as "Hi, I'm divorced Christi". Divorce may be something I have experienced, but it doesn't define who I am as a person. We are not our experiences. We tend to put labels on ourselves and as we continue to have painful or traumatic experiences, we put more labels on ourselves. We may think they define who we are, but that is only the case if we allow it to be so. As human beings, we have the right to our own choice and perception. Perception seems to be one of the only forms of truth—truth we accumulate through experiencing and choosing what we believe. When we are born, we are given the opportunity to reach our highest potential through experience. Healing the inner self allows us to return to the love from which we came and embody that in our physical self and spiritual being.

Letting Go of Labels

With this tool we address all of the labels we have placed on ourselves and those we have allowed others to place on us as well. The more you acknowledge and let go of, the better.

This tool is helpful in letting go of the labels you have placed on yourself and is helpful in identifying who you really are and your true value and worth. It is a very healing and empowering

Essential Oils recommended for this healing tool:

Cleansing Blend –

This blend of essential oils aids in releasing negative energy and toxic emotions. It allows one to clear their emotions out in order to make room for light, love, and positive energy. It aids in emotional breakthroughs past negative emotions allowing them to continuously progress towards clearing room for the new.

Joyful Blend –

This blend of essential oils is like a bright ray of sunshine in a bottle. It pierces through the darkness and clears the non-beneficial energy to make way for light and energy to travel to the heart and mind. It encourages one to dig deep within and realize the blessings and joy in life. It increases gratitude for life and experiences.

Calming Blend –

This calming blend is a blend that lovingly and tenderly reopens and heals the hurt or wounded heart. It softens one to open up others or the self and see the good. It encourages deeper healing to occur through forgiveness and releasing non-beneficial emotions which opens a place for love to enter and expand within the heart.

Bergamot –

This oil is an uplifting citrus oil that instills a sense of reassurance and confidence regarding the self. It aids individuals in recognizing their worth and value and to stand strong in their purpose. It allows them to lovingly view and accept their imperfections and to embrace themselves. It imbues confidence and allows one to let go of a lower belief in self. Through this oil they can see things with a greater confidence in self and purpose.

To purchase essential oils used in this book go to www.aromaheal.org

Exercise

(This exercise is recorded for your convenience and use. Please obtain your free download of the recording at <u>www.AromaHeal.org</u>.)

Set your intention before you begin this healing tool and say it out loud or in your mind.

"My intention is for healing to take place within myself using this powerful healing tool."

Lay down on your back with either your knees up or all the way down and close your eyes. We are going to go through a short breathing technique. Put a drop of Bergamot oil (or the oil of your choosing) in the palm of your hand and rub in a circular motion.

Cup your hands over your nose and take a deep breath in slowly to breathe in the aroma of the first oil and release your breath very slowly. **<u>Pause.</u>**

Take a second breath, relax your whole body and imagine you are in a world where only you exist in a space all your own. **<u>Pause.</u>**

Take another deep breath and slowly let it out and relax. Put your hands down and relax. Picture a really large jar. **<u>Pause.</u>**

Put all your worries for the moment into this big jar; everything that is weighing you down, stressing you out, or anything that is causing you anxiety or pain or taking your energy. Put it all in the big jar and then close the lid very tightly when you have everything contained in the jar. **Pause.**

Now picture a big shelf. Place the jar on the shelf and leave it there until you are done with this exercise and know that you can have it all back afterwards if you want. **Pause.**

Now continue with your eyes closed and picture yourself standing in front of a white board with a whole list of labels on it.

These are all the labels you have accepted about yourself. What are they? Step closer so you can see all of them and what they each say. These are all the labels that you have taken in and which you think define you. As we experience life, we take in false beliefs and we put labels on ourselves thinking that they define who we are. These are false beliefs we have accepted about ourselves.

Labels can be anything we put on ourselves. Things such as: broken, divorced, loser, fat, ugly, widow, victim, stupid, better than others, worthless, broke. Imagine the difference between saying I am divorced as opposed to saying I have experienced divorce or I am a widow as opposed to I have experienced my spouse dying. There is much power in the words "I am" and what we put after it.

Notice all the labels you have on you. Labels your parents put on you. If you are a mother or a father, what labels have you put on yourself that are associated with those roles? What about at work? What do your labels say? **Pause**. Now, picture a large container next to you and in it is a beautiful violet flame. This container is for you to put all the labels in and allow them to be engulfed by the violet flame. The flame is full of healing energy and a place to let go and release. **Pause.** Go through the process of taking every single one of the labels you have acknowledged off of the board and putting it into the violet flame. One at a time remove each one and release it into the violet flame. Watch them each disintegrate and burn until they are completely gone. **Pause.**

Now look on the board and make sure you have cleared and removed each one. **Pause.** Look at the white board and realize it is clean and clear and all that is left is YOU. Who are you without all these labels? Who are you without all the judgments you have put on yourself? You came to earth with a clean slate knowing exactly who you were, a precious and valuable creation. As a child you started allowing yourself to accept the labels others gave you. You now have a clean slate to create new feelings and experiences in your life. You are free of all those labels. No one has the power to create those but you. What do you want to create? Let's strengthen your connections and put positive affirmations in place of the old labels and beliefs. These are truths of who you really are and we are integrating these into your spirit so fully accept them. **Pause.**

Take a deep breath in and say to yourself in your mind:

> I AM whole.
> I AM connected to my higher power.
> I AM love.
> I AM worthy of love.
> I AM connected to myself.
> I AM connected to my purpose.
> I AM healed.

Now, take a deep breath in, and with your eyes closed, imagine looking in to your heart and visualize a white light growing within it and spreading from the center of your heart all the way out into your arms and legs and head. Engulf yourself in the feeling of peace and being cleansed and full of love.

Cup your hands over your nose and take a deep breath in slowly to breathe in the aroma of the oil again. **Pause.** Take 3 more deep breaths and inhale the oils and relax. **<u>Pause.</u>** To integrate your healing into your core, tap your stomach 3 times with your hand and say "Accept. Accept. Accept. Forever with me."

Testimonials

"I did the Healing Tool #2 and it was quite a freeing experience to let go of all the labels that I had put on myself. I didn't realize how much I was using labels as my identity. When I released all of them and threw them away, I felt a sense of freedom and a clean slate in me recognizing who I really was. I feel so free! I feel like I get to go out and decide who I want to be without all the labels."

We did this exercise as a group of women and it was amazing to see the healing take place! Afterward, several women shared how it felt to let go of some of the labels they had carried with them through their lifetime. One woman shared this: *"I didn't realize how long I had been carrying the label of being fat that I acquired from my father. He was a perfectionist to the hilt and wanted to correct everything. It always bothered him that I was heavier and he would tell me I needed to lose weight even as a little girl. I took it on as part of my identity that something was really wrong with me because I wasn't thin and perfect. I realize I literally fed into that as I got older and just always identified myself as fat and today I let go of that label and decided I am not my body. I am beautiful and amazing!"*

Another woman shared this: *"When I got divorced I felt like I was wearing a scarlet letter on my chest and I talked all the time about my divorce. It consumed me and I seemed to tell everyone about my horrible divorce. Years passed and as I was doing this exercise I realized how often I have let that be one of my labels where I introduce myself to people in single groups as "Hi! I'm Linda and I'm divorced. I've been divorced 7 years now." Now I'm changing it to Hi! I'm Linda and I love to have fun! Totally different feel to that! I don't have to be any of these labels! I can just be me and love me!"*

One woman expressed how different she felt after the exercise. She felt lighter and recognized how labels had defined her for too long. She cried with a sense of relief to know she was the one who got to define who she was and she could be whatever she wanted without anyone else defining it for her.

Healing Tool #3

Stress and Illness

Stress is a feeling of emotional or physical tension. It can come from any event or thought that makes you feel frustrated, angry, or nervous. Feelings from past experiences can cause stress and anxiety in the body. Stress causes deterioration in everything from your gums to your heart and can make you more susceptible to illnesses ranging from the common cold to cancer, according to a review essay in the Dec. 2007 issue of the Association for Psychological Science's magazine *Observer*.

In strictly medical terms, stress is your body's physical reactions to change, which is not always bad. It's the so-called "fight-or-flight" response that has been ingrained in our genetic codes since the earliest ages of our evolutionary ancestors: apes. In these early humans, stress helped people respond to life-threatening situations, such as man-eating animals.

Nowadays, your stress response might help you catch yourself if you trip, or steer your car to avoid an accident. But today's stress, especially when caused by psychological or emotional factors, can be prolonged and may have damaging effects on your health.

Stress can:
- cause sleep disorders, leaving you fatigued and more prone to accidents and illness.
- cause anxiety, nervousness and irritability, making it difficult to get along with people.
- affect your concentration, making you perform poorly at school or on the job.
- cause weight gain or weight loss.
- weaken the immune system, making you more susceptible to colds and other diseases, possibly even some types of cancer.
- spur you to abandon healthy habits, such as exercising and eating well, which may, in turn, create other health problems.
- be a contributing factor that makes digestive problems worse.
- be a key contributing factor in many health conditions, such as heart disease, high blood pressure, headaches, and arthritis.

These are concrete physical effects of stress, but they may be caused by stress that is either real or perceived. What this means is that people sometimes create unnecessary stress for themselves by worrying and fretting more than they should.[5]

Just as we can perceive stress, we can also dismantle those perceptions by using our mind to connect with the body and let go of the stress using pressure points and affirmations. The mind is a powerful tool. The following healing tool is useful and easy to use in any perceived stressful situation that may arise from a trigger of a past situation or traumatic event. The oils help to soothe the stress even further. This tool can be used to lessen the anxiety and stress level that kick in when triggers happen.

Short EFT with Aromatherapy

EFT stands for "Emotional Freedom Techniques", which was founded by Gary Craig in the 90's. It is a powerful self-help method, based on research, showing that emotional trauma contributes greatly to disease. Clinical trials have shown that EFT tapping is able to rapidly reduce the emotional impact of memories and incidents that trigger emotional distress. Once the distress is reduced or removed, the body can often rebalance itself, and accelerate healing.

EFT uses elements of Cognitive Therapy and Exposure Therapy, and combines them with Acupressure, in the form of fingertip tapping on acupuncture points. Over 20 clinical trials published in peer-reviewed medical and psychology journals have demonstrated that EFT is effective for phobias, anxiety, depression, posttraumatic stress disorder, pain, and other problems.[3]

This tool is very helpful with any given situation that may cause stress or anxiety and will help in lessening the power these situations have on you mentally and physically.

Testimonials

After a client of mine tried Healing Tool #3, she felt significant relief when she reflected on her past and the abuse she experienced that had previously caused her intense anxiety. She had anxiety around men and used this technique to calm her fears to the point that she no longer has them. She can't believe the difference she feels just by using this simple technique, along with the oils that make it more powerful and effective.

This tool can really be powerful for any potentially stressful situation that arises. One client used it before going in for job interviews and it helped him to completely relax and focus. He put the essential oils on his feet in the morning while getting dressed to calm himself and did the technique before going in to each interview and expressed how much calmer and more confident he felt while being interviewed and interacting.

Another woman expressed how she had PTSD and for years had taken natural supplements to help calm the anxiety that arose from all the related symptoms. She would walk in her sleep and have such strong reactions to dreams that her PTSD symptoms would kick in and she would literally have horrible accidents where she would walk through windows or end up physically hurt from harmful situations. The supplement worked for a while but then her body became so used to it that it was no longer effective. She was introduced to this really simple yet powerful modality and was amazed at the results. She stopped having horrible experiences while asleep and the symptoms of her PTSD decreased significantly. She still uses Healing Tool #3 often for any situation in her life that may cause her any stress or anxiety.

Exercise

(This exercise is recorded for your convenience and use. Please obtain your free download of the recording at www.AromaHeal.org.)

Choose one of your favorite Essential Oils:
- Lavender – refreshing, cleansing, freeing
- Eucalyptus – awakening, lifting, intelligence
- Frankincense – reflection, spirituality, expansion
- Melaleuca – antiseptic, anti-illness, healing
- Grounding blend– grounding, stabilizing, supporting
- Rose – loving, softening, forgiving, anti-grief
- Lemon – anti-fear, anti-stress, enlivening, rejuvenating

To purchase essential oils used in this book go to
www.aromaheal.org

Set your intention for this healing tool before beginning. For example: *My intention is to let go of stress in my body and to experience healing.*

Apply a few drops of essential oils to your outer ears and lobes, or diffuse. You can choose from the previous list or choose any other you may feel you need.

Find a nice and quiet space and sit down on a comfortable chair. Lay down if you wish. Uncross your legs.

Put a drop of essential oil in the palm of your hand and rub in a circular motion.

Think about what is bothering you and if you can feel it in your body. Is it anxiety? Are you stressed? Are you angry? Are you frustrated? Are you in pain? Are you feeling tired?

Pinpoint the feeling and get a little more specific: angry at boss, anxiety about a project, tired of this back pain, etc.

Cup your palms over your mouth and nose. Breathe in a few slow, deep breaths while imagining the issue or pain of the moment.

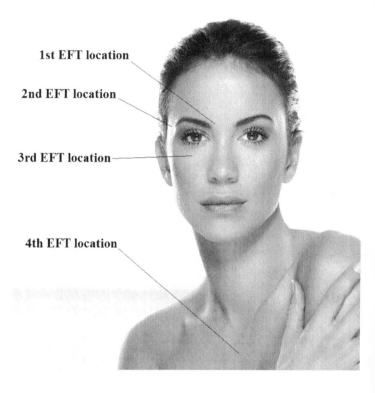

1st EFT location

2nd EFT location

3rd EFT location

4th EFT location

Start tapping with your forefinger right above the inner part of your eyebrow and say:
"This feeling I feel…"

Tap at the side of the eye while expressing the feeling - example:

"of being angry at my boss…"

Tap under your eye in the center at the top of your cheekbone and say:
"no longer serves me…"

Tap in the center below your neck right under the indentation of your neck on the collarbone and say:
"and I release it."

Repeat and do another round or two if necessary.

Now cup your aromatic palms over your mouth and nose and take a deep slow breath in and out to release it completely.

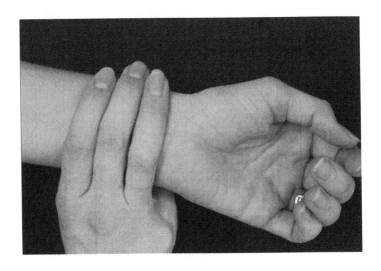

Take your 3 middle fingers of your right hand and place them over the front (palm side) of your left wrist and say "Peace" and hold it for 5 seconds.

Breathe in a few deep, slow breaths while acknowledging any changes in your body. Have your feelings reduced or shifted? Can you pinpoint any other issues that are bothering you at the moment? Are you calm?

Repeat the tapping process as desired for each emotion or event. Add more essential oil to your palms as needed or diffuse.

Healing Tool #4

Healing the Inner Self

The Inner Child

We can go along in life, experiencing the benefits of all the good changes we are implementing, feeling full of good, positive thoughts. Then once in a while, we have a hiccup, and we feel anger or react to something quickly in a negative manner. Or maybe it's a flashback, or a relationship that keeps popping up for us. Any number of things could put us back at a lower vibration and instantly we are triggered and pulled into the painful past.

There is a section of our psyche called the 'Inner Child'. It refers to a subordinate conscious that includes everything that happened to us as a child and pre-pubescent. Our Inner Child includes all of our emotions, experiences--good and bad--and beliefs that were instilled and learned. It guides our choices, actions, and emotions. Often, we carry false beliefs that we learned as a child with us throughout our lives. Healing the inner child can address issues such as abuse, addiction, trauma, and PTSD (Post Traumatic Stress Disorder). Past experiences of all degrees affect who we are as we age and shape us as adults.

The Inner Child represents the most innocent form of ourselves we are able to remember being. For most people, this child ceased to exist in the physical world when we were denied our right to freely express ourselves, by a parent, teacher, leader, etc. The Inner Child also holds our first perceptions of God and what God is. Therefore, God takes on many forms for different people, again, since our perceptions are formed from our experiences. This is important because it has to do with our understanding of self and what that means. Giving your Inner Child the right to freely express and be as you once were allows innocence and love to return to your being as a characteristic of yourself; no longer separate and kept within the dark confines of doubt and fear.

Therefore, healing the Inner Child is an important step. We as children have experiences that stand out to us as painful and hurtful because at a young age we did not have the reasoning, experience, and brain development we do as an adult. So with childlike thinking, some experiences have traumatized us as a child. Those memories and painful experiences are still inside of us. Then as adults, when we experience something that is sometimes totally unrelated, it triggers the pain of these childhood experiences to surface and we react to the pain and lash out in anger or frustration, etc. It is important to go back and heal those parts of our spirit that were hurt or traumatized, so that we no longer carry those experiences with us.

Even as teenagers, and then as adults, we have experiences that cause us trauma and pain. As we continue to hold onto those things, they deplete us of our energy. If we don't heal, let go, and forgive, they continue to wear on us and don't allow us to feel complete joy, happiness, and wholeness.

Reconnecting Our Spirit

This next exercise is a powerful tool in healing ourselves from the past experiences that continue to bring us pain and it is a powerful tool in giving ourselves what we need in order to heal. What is great about this tool is that we do not have to relive trauma or painful experiences in order to completely heal from them.

This exercise is most beneficial in a quiet place where you will be undisturbed. It's important you feel free to allow your emotions to come to the surface as you experience the wonderful healing this tool can give you.

This is a good exercise in helping to heal the parts of your spirit and soul that have experienced loss, grief and traumatic events.

Essential Oils used in this exercise:

Rosemary –
Rosemary essential oil is a powerful cleanser of non-beneficial energy and aids in creating a flow of energy. This flow of beneficial energy helps create a healthier transition between changes and disruption from life experiences. We sometimes absorb non-

beneficial energy because of these changes. Rosemary supports one to be able to smoothly move and transition from one experience to another while cleansing and releasing the non-beneficial energy and creating a space for new experiences and beneficial energy to exist.

Ylang Ylang –

Ylang Ylang is an emotionally uplifting, yet calming oil that elicits and initiates a beautiful opening up of the heart. This oil promotes the release of hard, built-up emotions that may have surrounded the heart in an effort to 'protect' it. Ylang Ylang instills a sense of trust, faith, and joy as a young child once again; igniting a passion and a purpose for life and living it to the fullest.

Geranium –

Geranium essential oil has the ability to mend the broken heart and allow one to love and feel love more fully. It encourages reception to trust, love, and reconnection with others when a loss or break in trust in the relationship has occurred.

Melaleuca –

Melaleuca essential oil allows one to break negative ties in relationships so that new, healthy ones can emerge. It encourages one to clear all forms of self-betrayal. It aids in releasing toxic debris and purifying the self.

Additional Oils Recommended for Use With This Exercise: (Choose which ones best suit you)

White Fir –

White Fir essential oil allows the self to realize and release negative false beliefs that have been passed on from one generation to another and releasing the cycles from continuing to repeat themselves.

Thyme –

Thyme essential oil is a powerful emotional cleanser. It cleanses the body and soul of negative emotions that have been buried deep within and opens up to allow the individual to fill themselves with love and light.

Cleansing Blend –

This essential oil blend helps to release toxic, non-beneficial emotions within the soul such as hate, rage, and anger and negative habits or patterns. This cleansing blend removes the negative out of our way to allow for the healing, clean energy to enter.

To purchase essential oils used in this book go to: www.aromaheal.org

Exercise

(This exercise is recorded for your convenience and use. Please obtain your free download of the recording at www.AromaHeal.org.)

Before beginning, set your intention for this healing tool. For example: *I am setting the intention that I find peace and healing in my life by applying this healing tool in my life.*

The amount of time it takes for this exercise varies for each person depending on what comes up for them so allow yourself at least 20-30 minutes to fully complete it.

Before beginning, apply essential oils to the feet and Ylang Ylang and Rosemary topically to the liver area on the abdomen. We process every emotion, particularly anger, through the liver, and often through the emotional heart as well. Any other oils you may want to use, rub on your feet.

Sit for a moment and ponder what experiences seem to keep coming up for you that were painful and you can't seem to quite let go of. Did things happen in your childhood that you feel you need to release in order to feel whole and move forward? Can you think of any age in your teens or adulthood that was particularly difficult for you? Just relax and think of any events that might have been traumatic and need healing. Ponder it for a few minutes and then go on to the following activity. **Pause.**

Loss Timeline

A powerful tool we can use in the realization of these painful, difficult, traumatic, or challenging experiences is to make a loss timeline.

Take a blank piece of paper and lay it horizontally in front of you and draw a horizontal line across a sheet of paper lengthwise and on one end mark "0" and on the other mark the age you are now. In the middle of the line, mark your halfway point between zero and the age you are now. For example, if you are 40, your halfway point will be at age 20. Start with your earliest recognition of your memories and how old you were at that age of your earliest recognition. Write down the year, age, and what that memory was. As you go through this exercise, write down any ages you remember and any losses or traumatic events up until the present moment. Record the year and the age you were at the time of the event so that you are aware of the time period and age you were that you need to heal.

For example: Say I had a serious illness at age 5. Then, at age 8 my parents got divorced. At age 16 I had a bad break up with a boyfriend that really hurt me. At age 27 I had a miscarriage and age 32 I got divorced. I would mark those and list them like this:

| 0 | 5 | 8 | 16 | **20** | ~ | 27 | 32 | ~ | ~ | **40** |

Age 5 – Serious illness
Age 8 – Parents got divorced
Age 16 – Bad breakup with boyfriend
Age 27 – Miscarriage
Age 32 – Divorce

You could have any number of ages that you came up with.

When you feel complete with this list of the traumatic events in your life, you are now ready to begin the healing part of the exercise. Keep this paper beside you as you do this exercise for a reference and reminder of the ages that you are healing within yourself.

Now close your eyes and picture yourself outside standing in a beautiful meadow. The grass is green. The sun is shining. The sky is blue and this meadow is beautiful and peaceful.

While closing your eyes, picture yourself at the different ages that you wrote down. If it was you at age 5 that had a traumatic or painful experience, then picture yourself at the age of 5 standing in that meadow in front of you. **Pause**.

Call to the other parts of you that were also traumatized--the 8 year old and 16 year old and each age that you wrote down. Picture yourself at each of those ages and see them standing in front of you in the meadow. **Pause.**

A version of you may appear at an age you don't even remember having a painful experience, but they also need this. Allow them to be a part of this wonderful healing experience with you.

Now, picture them all standing in front of you in that beautiful meadow. **Pause.**

Start with the youngest part of you and call him or her to you. It's not necessarily important to know what the pertinence of the loss was, because sometimes we can't even recall the experience. The important thing is that we heal this part of you so that you can feel whole and complete. As you call the youngest part of you that needs healing, have them come to you and stand directly in front of you. **Pause.**

Ask that child or part of you to tell you what it is that they needed and didn't get, or what they need from you in order to heal. In this moment you have everything in you and all the magic and all the power and access to anything they need in order to heal. Realize there are no limitations. As they tell you what it is, give them what they need. It could be unconditional love, reassurance, safety, affirmations, the need to be held and nurtured, or anything. Whatever it is they need, give it to them fully and freely until they feel complete. Spend a little time with them doing this. Allow the tears to flow if you feel emotional. **Pause.**

After this is done, call in your higher power, which is the God of your understanding, whomever or whatever it is that you identify as your creator and higher power, and call upon them to put a blessing of complete healing upon this part of you. As they put that blessing of healing upon this part of you, watch that part--the child, teenager, or adult--start to fill with light. Their whole being is healing and filling with the purest white and healing light, full of love. Every part of their being and every cell and every area of their being is being healed. You will know as soon as they are completely healed and whole. **Pause**

After this is complete, have that part of you once again stand in front of you. Hold their hands and look into their eyes. Have them say "I forgive and let go completely." Feel the release of granting forgiveness and letting go. Then, as you look into their eyes you are going to download everything into them that has occurred in your life from that age up to the present moment. As you do, they will grow before your eyes until they are the same age and height as you are now. **Pause**

As you look into their eyes when they are now the same height and age and person you are today, you are going to hug them and take them into you until they meld into you and become a part of you. Now, that part of you is whole and healed. Go back and do this with as many parts of you and at as many ages as you need to until you feel that you have taken each part into you now as you are in present day, and become more whole with each one.

Now, take Geranium essential oil to help in this healing process and hold it under your nose so you can breathe in the peaceful healing energy it can bring. As you feel this wholeness, I want you to silently say to yourself as you breathe in "I feel whole and I am at peace."

Do this exercise with each part of you that is standing in the meadow until you feel complete in bringing them all into you for a feeling of wholeness.

Do you feel more whole and at peace? The beauty of this tool is the power that we have to heal ourselves and give ourselves the needs that were not met by others. It is a beautiful and powerful tool for healing.

Any time you feel something come up from the past and the age you were at when you experienced this, use this tool to heal yourself and rid yourself of the pain it caused. Use it as many times as you need for each age or experience in your life.

Testimonials

"Some things that have been weighing on my heart and soul for my lifetime were literally lifted within just a couple of hours. This is something I have been working to do for years but had been unsuccessful until working with Christi. I am so excited to move forward without carrying that additional weight around on my mind and in my heart. Christi is truly gifted!"

"At first I had a hard time knowing what ages to go back to, I don't know if I was blocking them because some were so painful to me or what but once I sat and got really quiet with myself, I actually had several ages come to mind that I needed healing from. I think using the essential oil helped to calm me and helped me relax a little more. I even played some soft music to kind of help me relax even more and get my mind in a place that was open to seeing where I needed to heal. After I took the time I needed to do my timeline, I just sat and reflected for a little while and then I did some slow deep breathing to prepare myself. This tool took longer than the others but I see a deeper sense of healing in it too and felt so much lighter afterward. I went through each age I needed healing in and got stuck a little in trying to picture myself at some of the ages I needed to but once I

really relaxed and got quiet, I could finally focus and easily see myself at those ages. Each time I healed a part of me at a different age, I felt lighter. In one of the ages, I let the tears flow as I let go and allowed myself to heal. This tool was really pivotal in my healing and I was thankful to do it. It was like I gave myself my own power to heal and didn't have to rely on someone else to do it for me. I feel so much better and definitely lighter! I love this tool and I know I will use it again when something else comes up for me." (She noted that it is much easier to have someone guide her through it as they read to her the steps and what to do, than it was to do it on herself at first.)

One night as I worked with a group of people with Healing Tool #4 to find inner healing, one woman shared with me that as she pictured herself as a little child who needed healing, she had a deep desire to spend time with that little child within her. So she imagined and pictured sitting down and giving that child her full attention and spending some time with her while doing this exercise. She took the time necessary to give herself the needs she had as a child that weren't met. She enjoyed going back to spend time with the little girls that were *her* at different ages and stages in her life and gained more insight into what she went through as a child. She expressed to me how empowered she felt to heal those parts of herself. She was surprised at the level of healing that took place in her after this exercise and expressed her gratitude for me sharing it with her. This exercise can be so healing without having to re-experience the pain caused by certain incidents.

Conclusion

Healing can be so freeing and is essential to moving forward. Have you ever been told to "get over it"? What does "get over it" actually mean? What is the "it" we are trying to get over? If we keep pushing down feelings, we keep affecting our minds and our body and we hinder our growth and healing. The beauty in these tools is how we are able to release without being traumatized or re-experiencing the past. Acknowledgement itself is very effective. Having tools to guide you through the healing process can be helpful in accomplishing this.

These tools can be used as often as needed for personal healing and can be transformational—even life changing for many. I have seen and been told of their deep impact as I've utilized them within my practice, with friends, peers, and many personally shared experiences.

Our hope is that this book can transform and impact each who reads and implements the techniques within it. As they share their experiences, they will be able to help those around them, and effectively create a domino effect of powerful emotional healing throughout the world.

We hope that you have found this book educational, informative, and helpful in areas of emotional healing as well as how impacting essential oils can be in your healing process and that you become proactive in implementing them in your life. Many clients of mine use them on a regular basis when an emotion or experience comes up that needs to be healed. As we stated before, there are and can be some very deep emotional experiences that may need further in depth healing through scheduling some energy healing sessions and personally working with you on a one on one basis to help you release them. We know that each tool can be empowering and beneficial for you and we are excited to share this information and these techniques with the world as we truly help individuals heal themselves and therefore in turn, help heal the world.

Visit us at our websites: www.theahealingcoach.com www.karisatomkinson.com.

The Healing Coach

Christi Turley Diamond has a background in psychology and working with people who have had real traumatic loss in their lives. She worked with clients for years that were grieving in a variety of ways. We are taught how to acquire things and relationships but not how to deal with loss. The way we deal with loss is usually taught to us by the way our parents or caregivers dealt with loss and many times this misinformation and legacy of mistakes is passed on from generation to generation. As a result, we never really grieve the losses in our lives or feel complete. This can leave a hole in our hearts that seems to gape open at times; we are often overcome with heart-wrenching grief that leaves us feeling hollow inside.

She went on to train with life coaches and learned a variety of modalities and was realizing that clients were doing a lot of the right things but what held them back from progressing forward were the false beliefs they were carrying with them. They might have great goals to make a fortune but somewhere in their belief system was the belief that they weren't worthy of money so somehow they would sabotage receiving money. Or another client would have patterns of getting into bad relationships and couldn't recognize why they kept having the same kinds of relationships over and over and they felt stuck. It all went back to their belief system and Christi recognized that clearing these old beliefs was a key factor to them finally becoming successful financially or in relationships or whatever area they were being held back in. She became very intuitive to finding where the problem might be and helping clients to clear and release so they could heal and move forward.

Through study and experience she also realized that emotions can get stuck in the body in a place where they have never completely processed and they lie stagnant keeping people from progressing and maturing in aspects of their relationship in areas they don't feel complete or ways in which they push love away.

What stems from not fully allowing ourselves to grieve or process our emotions is an incompleteness within ourselves, a pain that can eat away at us for years. Because of this pain, we rob ourselves of living in the moment and become prisoners to the hold the past has on us. We end up with anxiety over our future and the fear of losing something else, denying ourselves the opportunity to feel joy and peace and live in the here and now.

Through energy healing and using essential oils, Christi has seen lives change completely and people heal who have held onto things for over 20 years. She knows the work she does can literally be transformational and life changing. She has clients all over the country that she does phone sessions with an in an hour's time, she sees results they haven't seen sometimes in years of therapy.

Christi Turley Diamond is dedicated to helping people heal. As they do, they are able to let go, find their purpose and live their passions. She finds her life work very fulfilling and feels privileged in doing it. She knows that God does all the healing and she has the honor of being the instrument to facilitate that. She helps people release blocks that hold them back. She clears emotional blocks regarding relationships, money, health and many others. She is the bridge from where you are to where you want to be and she coaches you in clearing barriers and then getting to your desired destination. Here are a few testimonials from those who have experienced her healing sessions:

"Few people allow their senses to guide their lives and even fewer take their gifts and share it with others. Christi Turley Diamond is one such person. Christi is a supportive teacher and a trust-worthy confidant. Her spiritual insight and training have allowed me to make progress in my life. I have made great strides in forgiving, processing loss and developing hope. I sailed through life more by chance than plan, never sure why I reacted the way I did to situations. I avoided looking too close at my past because the loss and pain were simply too great. In my simplistic way of handing things, I blamed myself for my poor choices and lived my life consumed with regret and avoidance. Through some emotional excavations, I realized I had carried learned traits from my childhood into my relationships. Christi has helped me to recover my memories, analyze the past, process the pain and learn to forgive and bring healing to past experiences I thought could never feel healed from. She introduced me to some powerful tools I could use in order to heal any relationship I still needed closure in. I no longer need to live in a state of avoidance and regret. I can now have hope and peace. Life is a journey; Christi is helping me navigate successfully through the roadblocks and enjoy the trip." -TerryKay D.

"Christi Turley Diamond is a true gift to this world where so many are hurting. Her ability to inspire clients and audiences to become more, to overcome obstacles and to truly connect to their highest self, is nothing short of miraculous. I recommend her to anyone who is seeking the light in their lives, who feel broken, down and out, and those who are not living up to their immeasurable privileges. To coach with her is to take a quantum leap in the right direction!" -Lisa Walker, creator of *Transform Your Results* International Speaker and Author

"Christi has empowered and assisted me during some of my most difficult times. She has real life experience, education and a gift for helping people regain clarity and most importantly HOPE in times of crisis. She has successfully walked me through my grief during times of darkness that I felt were impossible to get through. Christi has been a powerful guide in my journey to reconnecting to my authentic self, recognizing what my dreams and goals are and taking practical steps towards living a life I love." -Ang B.

"Christi has one of the most endearing personalities ever. She truly cares about people and wants each of us to discover who we are and make our own happiness. She has been on both sides of the spectrum and is truly the definition of turning tragedy into triumph. She graciously passes on the skills and tools she has learned along the way to becoming happy to those around her. Christi will help you set goals, motivate you and encourage you along the way to discovering your own path in life." -Liz C.

"Christi has a gift for seeing the blocks in others that hold them back from becoming who they can be. She took the time to help me see those in myself and discover that I was allowing too many things to keep me from my purpose and the life I have always wanted. She understands people on a deep level and has a gift of making it so easy to talk to her and share those things about me that are sometimes hard to admit. I was able to sit and accomplish goals I had never been able to do. I was able to move forward and really heal after I applied the tools that she shared with me. She helped me to empower myself and push forward and I am becoming the man I have always wanted to be. I am grateful for the coaching I have received from her and how it has changed my life!" - R. B.

"Christi came into my life as an angel. She has such a deep insight into people and their feelings. I would go as far as to say that she literally saved my life. I was at such a low point in my life that I was at the point of contemplating taking my life. She pulled me out of the deep hole I was in. She made me feel like I mattered and that my life and what I did with it mattered. Even though she hasn't been through everything I have, somehow I could sense that she really understood me and she talked to me in a way that I know she really cares about me and about people. I could talk to her in a way that I couldn't with anyone else and it made all the difference. I started doing positive things with my life and started seeing purpose and meaning again. I'm so grateful for this angel God gave to me and I am here today because of it." -Sherri M.

Christi Turley Diamond B.S., M.Ed. is a Grief Recovery Specialist, an Energy Healer and Life Coach. She facilitates sessions over the phone with clients nationwide. If you have experienced loss in any way or you just feel stuck and want a way out or need to delve further into deeper healing and are seeking some answers on how to heal and feel whole, you can schedule a session with her on her website at www.thehealingcoach.com.

Essential Oils

Necessary Essential Oils for Healings Tools 1-4:

- Ginger
- Clove
- Melaleuca
- Oregano

- Bergamot
- Rosemary
- Ylang Ylang
- Geranium

Additional Essential Oils Recommended:

- Cleansing Blend
- Joyful Blend
- Calming Blend
- Lavender
- Eucalyptus
- Frankincense

- Grounding Blend
- Lemon
- Rose
- White Fir
- Thyme

To purchase essential oils go to www.aromaheal.org

References

1. LeDoux, JE, *Rationalizing Thoughtless Emotions*, Insight, Sept. 1989

2. Mein, Carolyn L, D.C.. *Releasing emotional patterns with essential oils*. Santa Fe: Vision Ware Press, 1998

3. Bodymind. (2014, September 8). Retrieved September 10, 2014, from http://en.wikipedia.org/wiki/Bodymind

4. Shakeshaft, J. (2014, July 2). 6 Breathing Exercises to Relax in 10 Minutes or Less. Retrieved from http://greatist.com/happiness/breathing-exercises-relax

5. Levine, J. (n.d.). Can Stress Kill You? Retrieved September 1, 2014, from http://www.askmen.com/sports/health/25_men s_health.html

6. EFT- Emotional Freedom Techniques. (2013, January 1). Retrieved from http://www.eftuniverse.com/

7. *Emotions & Essential Oils: A Modern Resource for Healing* (2nd ed.). (2013). American Fork, UT: Enlighten Alternative Healing, LLC.

8. Fish, M. (1999). *Healing the Inner Self: From Darkness Into Light*. West Pacos Lane Trust.

9. MacDonald, D. (2012). *Emotional Healing With Essential Oils* (2nd ed.). American Fork, UT: Enlighten Alternative Healing, LLC.

10. *Modern Essentials: A Contemporary Guide to the Therapeutic Use of Essential Oils* (5th ed.). (2013). Orem: AromaTools.

Christi Turley Diamond B.S., M.Ed., is a Speaker, Energy Healer and a Life Coach. She worked for years in a non-profit organization working with many affected by loss and trauma and providing services to support them in their healing. She obtained several awards for her work with the organization. She now works from her own office and loves to connect with her clients all over the country in Energy Healing sessions and Life Coaching over the phone. She has been trained in a variety of modalities and says that she pulls from her "energetic toolbox" in each session she does. She has worked with hundreds to help them heal. She has her Bachelor's degree in Psychology and her Master's degree in Instructional Design/Education. She has been teaching in a variety of ways for many years and enjoys educating others about the healing properties of pure essential oils. It is her passion to help others let go of pain in order to serve their purpose. Her purpose is to bring healing to the world. You can find her on her website at www.thehealingcoach.com. When she is not doing sessions, she is spending time with her 4 amazing children and her supportive husband. She loves to travel, dance, and have fun!

Karisa Tomkinson B.S., M.S., is an Occupational Therapist and a wellness advocate currently residing in Ohio. Health is an important aspect of her lifestyle. Her work in Occupational Therapy has enlightened her with valuable knowledge about the body and what is necessary for it to function at its optimum level by what you put into it and how you physically take care of it. She loves working one on one with patients and empowering them in their lives through the therapy she provides. She began using essential oils as they complemented her studies and knowledge as a therapist and has grown in her passion for the healing and emotional aspect they provide. She has designed and managed her own retail store and is a photographer, but mostly loves her work mentoring and coaching a business team that spans coast to coast. You can learn more about her on her website www.KarisaTomkinson.com. She and her husband have two kids and in her free time she enjoys road biking, long distance running, and being outdoors. She is outgoing, devoted to her faith and family, and lives her life on purpose!

Made in the USA
San Bernardino, CA
05 March 2016